REQUIEM

REQUIEM

A LAMENT FOR THE DEAD

KWAME DAWES

PEEPAL TREE

First published in Great Britain in 1996
Peepal Tree Press Ltd
17 King's Avenue
Leeds LS6 1QS

21/9/09

ISBN 1 900715 07 4

The poems in *Requiem* were inspired by the illustrations
of Tom Feeling in
The Middle Passage: White Ships/Black Cargo

To Lorna, Sena, Kekeli and Akua

Won't you help to sing
These songs of Freedom
'Cause all I ever had
Redemption songs

Bob Marley

CONTENTS

RESEARCH

... for me that was New York City, that was where the pain was.

Tom Feeling,

You did not have to imagine
the masks of agony,
did not have to research
the eyes' blank stare,

Did not have to study ethnic tribes
to see the shape of Africa
in the lips and noses
the weight of buttocks,

Did not have to invent
the blues of suffering,
the jazz of rebellion,
the fire of survival,

'Cause you looked across
Brooklyn and saw the road-weary
gaze of them who still travel
in the belly of ships,

Them who still sit among the cinder,
the soot, riding that freedom train
to the factories of the North
herded into the tombs of the ghetto;

Stared at your face in the mirror
after the stomach unfurls,
the skin smarting from being
spat on, shat on, pissed on.

9

You draw lines from somewhere cherished;
our gasps, groans, whispers
are the minor-keyed, antiphonal melodies
of our recognition of self.

We enter your holocaust
with trepidation and leave the stench
with tears, and something like gratitude
for the waters of healing, the salt, the light.

BIRD FLIES

bird flies

I have not known peace,
not known mornings
like bird flight.

I have not woken
to a shrine
ancient as my skin,
to the scent of offered blood.

I search my memory
for icons of remembrance;
coke bottles, washboards,
nets woven in raked soil
for new grass, my signs.

I have dreamt
of something beyond
the clamour of this city,
dreamt of robust youth
sprinting through the savannah.

bird flies

I have not known peace,
not known mornings
like bird flight.

There is a soft saxophone
choking on its own sound,
making like a bird in flight

when you close your eyes.
Open them to see the whites
of a Black man's eyes

searching you for something
lost, blowing in sharp
bursts from his tender
lips, white eyes chained
to the trembling glass
of rot-gut, no ice –

bird flies

I have not known peace,
not known mornings
like bird flight;
no one's flying these days.

FIRST KILL

Garth, my neighbour,
stands on Gun Boat beach,
eyes peering far to the horizon
filmed with something like tears;
in this half-light of morning,
the fishermen, slow as dreams,
pushing a scar across the beach,
drop and rise on the placid water...

Garth tells of a first kill,
kneeling in the middle of some
downtown street, stark of light,
faceless homes, lining up the boy,
black boy sprinting, tossing back
bullets like stones missing
everything in his wake, mad runner,
then a sudden explosion is all.

How treacherous a tiny pellet
hurled through the air, how it makes fall
a grown man. In his eyes,
you see a startled stare,
telling you that deep down
he knows, like you, that man
was not made to be felled by
sightless stones, man was made
to die by the intimate machete's swing.

Garth has tasted first blood.
Casual as a confessional box,
our temple of regret is closed.
The sea contains the secrets
spoken by bullet-pierced thousands.
We listen for the cry of anger:
nothing comes back but the caw
of sea gulls, and the tick of surf.

TRAIN COMING

The trees unfurl like twisters
flooding the sky with black;

in the glare of lightning
the train slumbers by

at the human pace
of dragged, unwilling feet.

From far, the whistle blows;
from another country the whistle

blows me homewards, the sounds
of the train, breathing, grunting,

keeping pace with the crunch
of leather soles on gravel,

the echo of thunder. When the clouds
open and rain tiny dots

how we howl, how we howl!
Through the night there is light

and the faint glimmer of a lake
too broad, too long...

The train crawls into new spaces
to the crunch of leather soles.

CRIME OF PASSION

The baobab tree, implacable witness,
to the smashing of what little we had,
does not offer shelter. I inscribe

these revelations in words that search
for a song in the faceless shadows
of the men who string my ankles,

drag me here. Oh to stay in the simple
dialectic of hatred and brutality
there at the edge of my flaming hut,

to remain in that fire-bright place
of purest hate, the stranger, a beast,
my fist clear-eyed, pounding life

from his faceless howls. All this long before
the gospel of crosses, blood; the song
of promised lands I have embraced,

long before I copulated
with his books and gave birth to words,
long before he found my tongue,

could sing with my tongue, owned my tongue
while I toyed with his. Now my fist
is a cataracted beast, unable to shake

the monkey of affinity from my back.
Neurotic me, when once all was simple
passion, now I cannot kill without premeditation,

16

cannot act without the legacy of that baobab
staring mutely at the ravage of my hut
before time, before time, before time.

WOMB

Have you seen my womb
on pitch black nights,
the way the trees spread
like tendrils of fallopia
trying to suck in the stars?
Have you seen the mess
of dry black blood,
my old flow clotting?

In a simple tree
where a village once stood –
they could tell from the circles
of burnt straw in rows for miles around –
they found a spear lodged,
the blade rusted red,
the wood weather-worn and light,
and no one dared to touch
the sanctity of the moment.

When the spear flew
it did not flame
or find its mark,
it merely pierced
the trunk of the tree,
impotent and vulnerable
like the flame-chewed
belly of our village.

SWAMP POEM

Sometimes, in the mist,
the artist can see the shape
of soldiers tense with waiting,
their guns at the ready.

The mist dries quickly
as the heat of the day comes,
and the artist is sitting
in the still of a swamp.

Outside Sumter, he buys boiled
groundnuts, feels his heart
thumping, his stomach heaving –
for a while there, in the mist,

he thought he smelt
the dank scent of kenke,
thought he was in Ghana
before the sun came.

Out of the lifting white
a boat glided by,
a woman, worn with age
nodded her black head, passing.

The artist works quickly
in charcoals, fingers turning black,
eyes turning back to the swamp
to the mist, to another life.

LINES

White lines
stretched on black
they wait in silence;
it is pre-dawn.

Above, the storm gathers;
this is a nightmare
drawn in fingers
stained with charcoal,
smudging away the flames.

They return stark
the white of the page
resisting the brush of dark.

White flames lick;
the village is eaten.

REQUIEM

I sing requiem
for the dead, caught in that
mercantilistic madness.

We have not built lasting
monuments of severe stone
facing the sea, the watery tomb,

so I call these songs
shrines of remembrance
where faithful descendants

may stand and watch the smoke
curl into the sky
in memory of those

devoured by the cold Atlantic.
In every blues I hear
riding the dank swamp

I see the bones
picked clean in the belly
of the implacable sea.

Do not tell me
it is not right to lament,
do not tell me it is tired.

If we don't, who will
recall in requiem
the scattering of my tribe?

In every reggae chant
stepping proud against Babylon
I hear a blue note

of lament, sweet requiem
for the countless dead,
skanking feet among shell,

coral, rainbow adze,
webbed feet, making as if
to lift, soar, fly into new days.

VULTURES

Companions of our march,
vultures can smell
the sour of death.

All instinct,
there is a simple patience
in their watch. Fallen,

the body still breathes.
Out of the corner of the eye
the slipping soul can see

the flutter of vultures
calmly waiting for the twitch
to slow to a smoothness.

They hop forward with each gasp,
circle, respecting the light of life
in the eye, then, quietly, they feast.

There is no other way back
to the kraal except by the giving
of final breath; death comes and then flight.

What is left is mere grotesquery;
but the vultures understand the simple
equations of ecology; theology eludes them.

Circling above, they track the lines,
footprints like train tracks,
that fade with the whipped wind.

23

These vultures speckle a blue sky
and learn the trade routes
to the castles by the sea;

they arrive, bloated, low-bellied
like Russian cargo planes,
and rest in the yard, sentinels

to this trade in carrion,
this scavenging of flesh,
this transporting of limbs.

They follow the thin trail
of the ship's cut, still smelling
the canker of a slaver,

but falter as the salt grows tart,
and the smell of earth dries up.
They can return to old haunts.

After a final circle
they fade into the horizon.
The ship slouches on.

COLLABORATORS

I dreamt last night
that the earth curled
like a wave shading me
and the day turned black.

In that dream
was a duppy army
wispy like cotton,
blown in the wind.

Sentinels stood
in sturdy relief,
black man with whip,
always the brother.

Burning spear flew from my hand,
wounding collaborators,
Now it is an old habit,
this spilling of my own blood.

Had a dream of a wave
gathering like a cloud
over me, old water and bones
falling on me, drowning me

CAVE

Above us is granite,
below us the give of wood
seasoned with constant blood,
piss, shit, vomit, sweat –
our essence seeping out of us.

We left our souls behind
in that last light of the courtyard
where two children stood
crying without tears.

We watched, as one, the way
our souls lifted with the stench
of our fear, trying to catch the current
back to the ancient shrine.

The children howled,
wooden shackles tethering them,
their nakedness a smudge
on the pale white of limestone.

We crawled, soulless, but with the suggestion
of song into our tomb. Beyond this is burial
repeated in ritual efficiency:
the cave, the hull, the strange ocean.

Sometimes in the blues
you sense a dry, hollow cry;
it is the wail from the granite cave
caught in mid-flight, mid-flight.

LANGUAGE

Ashantis, Mandingoes, Ibos, Wolofs, Fulanis, Coromantees
Ashantis, Mandingoes, Ibos, Wolofs, Fulanis, Coromantees

Buried in the hill country,
the swamp lands, the forests
of this New World oven
the words of tribes linger
like old mystery songs
tracing us back to something

Ashantis, Mandingoes, Ibos, Wolofs, Fulanis, Coromantees
Ashantis, Mandingoes, Ibos, Wolofs, Fulanis, Coromantees

COUNTY COUNCILLOR

Enthroned in the pomp of county governance,
the seasoned reverend is too short for his throne.
His flaxen head bobs above the ornate fencing
nodding at the tailored pronouncements of the chair,
old southern blood red against his hot neck.
Passer of laws, kisser of babies, sometimes
he walks through an avenue of black faces,
Christ among the sinners, offering promises.

The seasoned reverend glistens with weighty gold,
jangling his keys for the stretch cadillac,
plotting his Sunday sermon of brimstone,
sweat flowing like the holy ghost in his temple
where he is king, bossman, maker of dreams.
Here in this staid reverence of county ceremony
his self-importance overwhelms him, leaving him
feeling blacker than he ever did before, and shame.

How many brothers has he sold down the river
for that seat so low it swallows him,
for the humble ways he has learnt to get his bread?
How many sisters left to weave in the wind
for the pittance of glory he tastes from their tables?
I stare at the puppet head, bobbing, nodding,
grinning the Christian love he trades in,
enthralled by the strained rituals of power.

I have seen the fattened prosperity before,
the pragmatic splendour of conspicuous wealth.
All is in the transaction, the deals we make,
there is no blood in the green of money.
I travel to the West Coast of Africa, there
where the Atlantic's turbulence ravages the shore,
and see him hoisted on his throne, dealing powder,
rifles, cloth, trinkets for flesh. The smile is the same.

CROSS

At the helm of the boat
a cross to light them home.

Gail is gobbled by the lounge chair,
incongruous black softness in my office.
She gazes at the strewn pictures,
mute images of callous ways,
and calls herself a "Generation X"
who doesn't give a hoot what they want
to call her, 'cause she cares
but doesn't have to march to care.

She mutters at the open page,
"Their backs must have hurt.
For days, no movement; it would kill me."

At the helm of the boat,
parting the undulating sheets of white,
a cross to light them home.

"How could they go for months
like that, like that, like that?"

At the helm of the boat,
the ghost man counts the beat
of the oars' dip and rise
in the fluent Atlantic,
heading towards the tapestry
of ropes, masts, canvas —
the uneasy cutter waiting
against a muddy sky

a cross to light them home

"Amazing grace how sweet the sound"

RABID

Like the spittle of a rabid dog,
once it enters the blood,
is the smell of burned flesh,
the brand of iron on skin;
you stare at water
until the madness settles;
once sniffed, there is little else
for the slaughterer of flesh,
but stark muteness.

I see a vacuous silence
in your eyes of something
long left behind on some Scottish lea
long before the sea
and the taste of black flesh,
the sweat of slave women
eked out with screams
gave you appetites.

Muttering the litany of Psalms
each morning for safety at sea
and a burial in soft Highland loam,
I see you looking above
for that departing soul.
The depraved know themselves,
can smell the canker of their breath.

FAMILY TREE

My grandmother, she was light skinned,
could have passed for white,
but it was too dangerous,
and she talked like us.

I remember seeing her laid out
there, with all her white hair
like ribbons, on the red velvet
and somebody told me she was dead.

And I kept wondering how come
a white woman was laying in our house
making daddy bawl like that,
like I had never seen him bawl before.

Now her daddy, he was white,
but my daddy didn't know him,
saw him sometimes, but didn't know him.
And her mother, his grandmother,

she was black, she was a slave,
and the daddy, the white man,
he would go on and get his pleasures
from her till she would swell.

Now he was married, mind you,
but like folks always said,
them black slave womens, they had power,
something would make white men weak.

They had it good for a time,
on account of the fair-skinned boy,
but that black woman, she stayed
with a black old soldier for too long,

and it's like everything turned on her,
and the white man, he got mad
and they killed the soldier, straight like that.
That woman went mad. That's my family.

We still hates them somehow,
like something you born with in the blood,
but they still comes sniffing by.
I seen the way they come grabbing me

when I was a cook with them,
and I turn them away, cause they make my skin
crawl, when I think of how he forced her;
'cause he did — they always do, they do.

HATE

for Joseph Cinque and the Africans on the *Amistad*

I understand hate.
I used to know fear.

That flame in my eyes
Not madness, nothing so benign.

Just pure hate.
I could eat your heart   raw.

SHAME

If I heard the wail of a child,
over the lap of the sea,
heard the ebb of its whimpering,
eyes searching the void
for the familiar dark
of my face, my womb would burst,
my throat would open
and shatter the sky
with its scream.

They stand him
on wooden planks
to stare at the gawking heads
of men, too defiant
to make the passage to nowhere.
He stares, eyes tearing from the salt
in the humid air.
He must not hear me
stifling my moans,
numbing my flesh
from the stabbing
of those bloody penises

At night
the creaking of the boat
lulls the tomb
and the babies,
chests weary with howling,
moan in reverie
while we lick our wounds,
wipe the wet from our thighs,
avert our gaze from the shame
of men, still alive, now boys,
witnesses to our abuse.

ANCHOR

Let me drown
in the white
of the moon,

Let me open
my eyes and fall
into its silver belly,

Let me fade
into its depths
while I can still see

the tree-tops
of this land
of my navel string.

BURIAL AT SEA

The vultures of the seas
can smell the drip
of ebbing life
seeping through
the cracks in the wood.

It is morning;
before the hot of midday,
the ghosts walk through
unshackling the dead,
lifting the leather and bones.

No words spoken,
no libation,
just a ritual tossing
of bodies overboard,
the captain pricking his ledger.

Lloyd's will give sterling
for jettisoned cargo.
To round up the numbers
the whimpering sickly
are tossed into the ribbons of foam.

Now I can stretch my legs
my feet feel blood again;
the dead leave space
for the living.
The ancestors have forgotten us.

BALM

My brother, I have no words
to repeat the howl of the crippled land
at the amputation of a limb;
to describe the ghoulish masks of the earth
feeling the uprooting of trees,
the blood wail, neck straining;
to touch the arrow of a cutter
slashing its indiscriminate way
through the barren sea
bearing the fruit of the soil.

Can the spirits find a path
beyond the wall of silence
to find the children?

I stare at your lines, my brother
at their bas-relief of suffering,
and find written words are base.
I thought the blues could call up
the howl we heard when it happened,
but the blues are a lament;
this is a scream, that wrenching
unformed wail of a horn
howling, howling, hooowwwlllliiiing!

Can the spirits find a path
beyond the wall of silence
to find the children?

Who whispered these images into your eyes,
was it there in Accra, or maybe Tema?
Did they announce themselves discreetly,
or were there floods of weeping?

I send these words as a balm
for your livid soul, stretched
by this journey you have taken
all these years, for the pain in your bones,
the blood shed in the etchings.
I can only offer oils of healing
after the sweat and blood of birthing.

HOMELESS

Homeless, homeless,
The moonlight's fading on a midnight lake
Paul Simon

They massage us with words
we cannot understand
but can feel the coaxing,
as they pass the bowl of life
under our noses, to tempt us.

I know the embrace of water,
know that beneath the blue
are the spirits of my tribesmen.
I stare away from the food to the sea.

Then, tilting my head,
they force metal prongs
and twist the screw till my jaw
snaps, and life is poured in.

I feel for the loosening of their grip
at the softness in my throat,
hear the sigh of accomplishment;
then in the lapse, I leap.

I have flown, flown, eyes open wide,
and then the water, warm and embracing,
takes me, swallows me, long before
the tug of teeth on my limbs.

I come back only to say
that repeating the litany of pain
is a requiem to my memory.

Take me into your head again,
dance around the fire,
then raise the white hen high;
I will enter her and you will watch her
eyes dilate seeing the ocean's bottom.

There by the baobab tree
lay her down among the roots,
burn herbs for her, burn herbs.
I have floated too long without a home.

WARRIOR

1

Like a whip
unfurled,
his body
still taut
from sprinting
behind the fleeing elephant
gathers the ghost
and with a sudden plunge
guts the monster.
There is blood,
and the smell of bile.
The warrior
laughs, staring at the blood.
There is shock in his eyes
when they bring him down

2

Only to hoist
him up

3

Jerking,
jerking,
then still,
life is breathed out,
he dangles,
the warrior,

from the mast.
4

Before you look
you smell
the swelling flesh;
the salt makes leather
of his skin;
flies nurtured
in the meat
mask the white
of his eyes.

5

You think
the rotting
will cause the neck
to give, but the skin
is now leather;
the rope
finds the grooves
of the spine,
hooks in.

6

I see the thong
of his member
wither;
it falls.
The ghost

stares at the shrunken snake
as if staring at his own
manhood. Somebody laughs.

7

It is hard now
to smell the canker.
The wind blows through
him like a flag.
The body is gutted
by the turning gulls.

The watch cries
Land!

8

I leave my heart
with the dangling warrior

I leave my heart
with the dangling warrior.

His teeth grin back
at me.

RAT

This belly of the ship
is a tomb.

The rats clear the bones;
the skin dries.

They have forgotten
the curled-up body

of a baby long dead.
I cannot smell him,

I can only hear
the scratching of rats

dragging his bones
into their holes.

The rats never grow thin,
beasts in the belly of the whale.

LAND HO

I cannot speak the languages
spoken in that vessel,
cannot read the beads
promising salvation.

I know this only,
that when the green of land
appeared like light
after the horror of this crossing,

we straightened our backs
and faced the simplicity
of new days with flame.
I know I have the blood of survivors

coursing through my veins;
I know the lament of our loss
must warm us again and again
down in the belly of the whale,

here in the belly of this whale
where we are still searching for homes.
We sing laments so old, so true,
then straighten our backs again.

ABOUT THE AUTHOR

Kwame Dawes is part of a new generation of Caribbean writers grounded in a tradition which speaks of possibility. He draws upon inspiration as diverse as Derek Walcott, T.S. Eliot, Lorna Goodison, Bob Marley and Peter Tosh. He was born in Ghana in 1962, moved to Jamaica in 1971 where he remained until 1987. He has also lived in England and Canada. He now lives in America where he is Professor of English at the University of Columbia. Kwame is an accomplished broadcaster, actor, dramatist and reggae musician. He has published five collections of poetry, *Progeny of Air*, (Peepal Tree Press, 1994), *Resisting the Anomie* (Goose Lane Editions, 1995), *Prophets*, (Peepal Tree Press, 1995), *Requiem* (Peepal Tree Press, 1996) and *Jacko Jacobus* (Peepal Tree, 1996). *Progeny of Air* won the Forward Poetry Prize for the best first collection of 1994. Kwame is married to Lorna and they have three children, Sena, Kekeli and Akua.

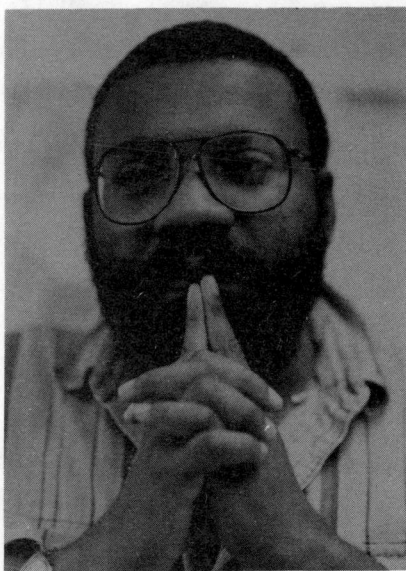

ALSO BY KWAME DAWES

Prophets

As 24-hour television, belching out the swaggering voices of American hellfire preachers, competes with dancehall, slackness and ganja for Jamaican minds, Clarice and Thalbot preach their own conflicting visions.

Clarice has used her gifts to raise herself from the urban Jamaican ghetto. She basks in the adulation of her followers as they look to her for their personal salvation. Thalbot has fallen from comfort and security onto the streets. With his wild, matted hair and nakedness, he is a deranged voice in the wilderness. Whilst Clarice has her blue-eyed Jesus, Thalbot brandishes his blackness in the face of every passer-by. Clarice's visions give her power; Thalbot is at the mercy of every wandering spirit. But when, under cover of darkness, Clarice 'sins' on the beach, Thalbot alone knows of her fall. He sets out to journey, like Jonah, to denounce the prophetess and warn the Ninevite city of its coming doom. An epic struggle begins...

Brag Magazine wrote '*Progeny of Air* reads like the opening communication from a writer of major significance'; *Poetry Review* said 'I look forward to seeing what *else* this man can do.' Here in *Prophets* that promise is delivered. *Prophets* is an epic poem of vast energy and pace, multi-layered richness and allusive wit. In *Prophets*, Kwame Dawes has written a humane comedy of spiritual striving which will surely be recognised as one of the major works of the decade.

ISBN 0948833 85 8
Price £6.95
160 pages